THE GREAT STATE OF
TEXAS

With love from,
Ann & Fernando
6-15-89

THE GREAT STATE OF
TEXAS

PHOTOGRAPHY BY REAGAN BRADSHAW
TEXT BY GRIFFIN SMITH, JR.

GRAPHIC ARTS CENTER PUBLISHING COMPANY
PORTLAND, OREGON

International Standard Book Number 0-912856-96-3
Library of Congress Catalog Number 85-071191
Copyright © 1985 by Graphic Arts Center Publishing Company
P.O. Box 10306, Portland, Oregon 97210 • 503/226-2402
Editor-in-Chief • Douglas A. Pfeiffer
Designer • Robert Reynolds
Cartographer • Thomas Patterson
Typographer • Paul O. Giesey/Adcrafters
Printer • Graphic Arts Center
Bindery • Lincoln & Allen
Printed in the United States of America
Second Printing

Frontispiece: The hardy Texas longhorn
was better suited for the rugged
trail drives of the 1870s than the
close quarters of today's feedlots.
Right: The agave is often called
the century plant because it
blooms so rarely.

To Elizabeth Bradshaw

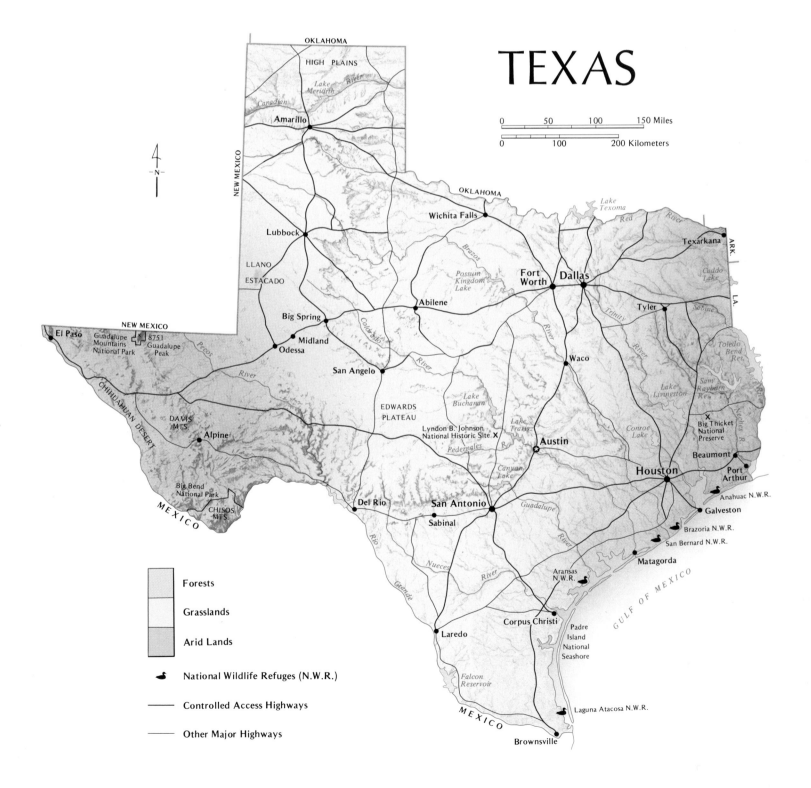

TEXAS

0   50   100   150 Miles

0   100   200 Kilometers

Forests

Grasslands

Arid Lands

National Wildlife Refuges (N.W.R.)

Controlled Access Highways

Other Major Highways

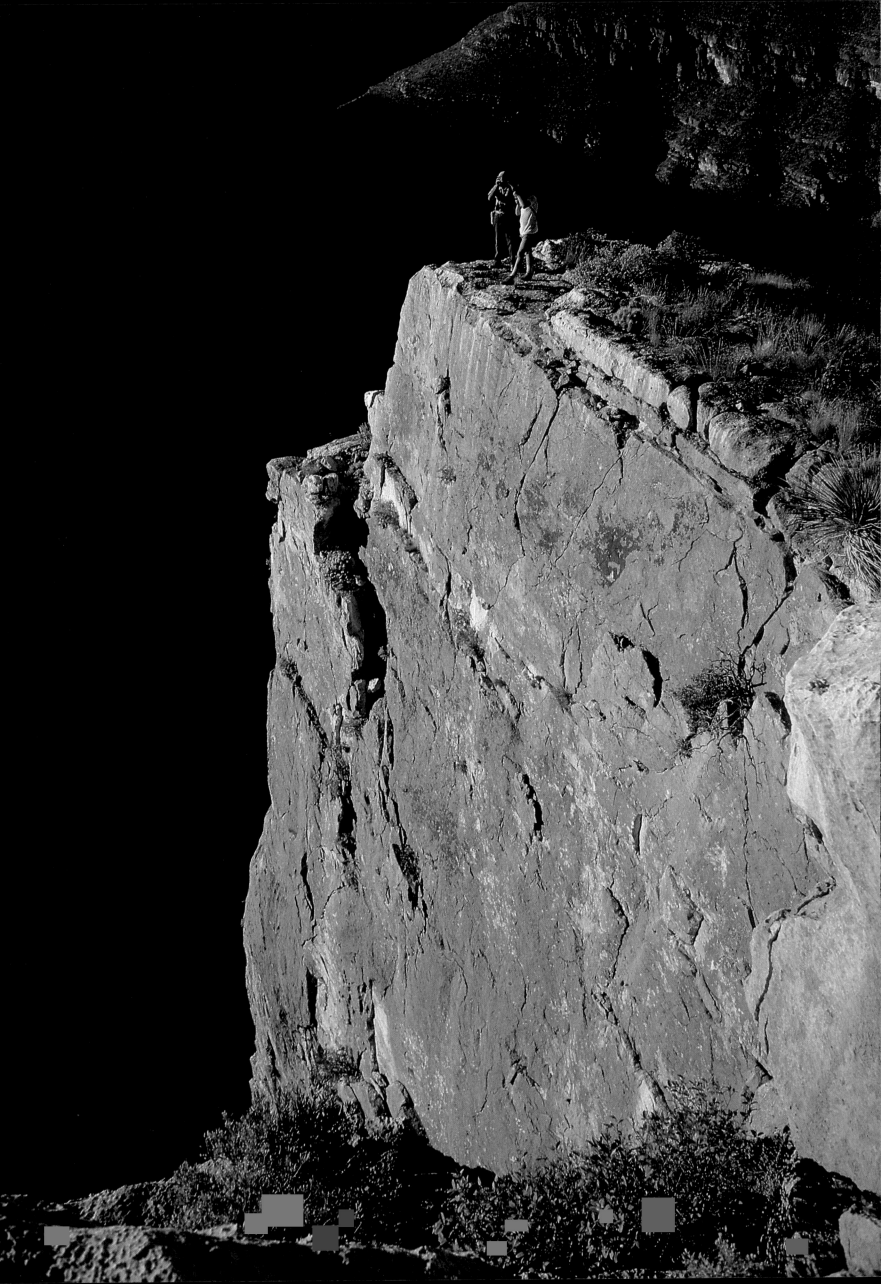

Left: The Rio Grande, two thousand feet below Burro Bluff. *Above:* Twenty-five miles long, some fifteen hundred feet deep, Boquillas Canyon offers spectacular scenery in Big Bend National Park. *Overleaf:* The Alamo. In 1836, 187 Texas defenders held off five thousand Mexicans for eleven days before they were overrun. Seven weeks later troops shouting, "Remember the Alamo!" triumphed at San Jacinto, the decisive battle in the Texas War for Independence.

Two combines cut through amber waves of grain at harvest time near Perryton, the northernmost town in the Panhandle. Texas wheat country in the north Panhandle lies adjacent to the Oklahoma Panhandle and less than forty miles from Kansas. Amarillo, which lies south, is the heart of the Cattle Kingdom.

The Hill Country. The barbed wire fence changed Texas history. Within a decade of its introduction in the 1870s, the open range had disappeared, the great trail drives had ended, and fence cutting was a felony. This post was hewn from native cedar, which is sturdy and durable enough to withstand extremes of climate.

The spring-fed rivers of the Hill Country northwest of San Antonio run clear and cold through limestone beds. This cowboy, the epitome of western solitude, is crossing the Medina River near Bandera, a center for dude ranches.

The bluebonnet, or buffalo clover, is the Texas state flower. It blooms for a month in the early spring and since ancient times has been cultivated in many parts of the world to enrich the soil. The Brenham area, site of this pasture, is one of the choicest locations in the state for viewing the display.

This palm frond in Santa Ana National Wildlife Refuge is typical of the vegetation found in natural areas near the lower Rio Grande, where subtropical forest mingles with native brush. The Rio Grande rises in southwest Colorado and flows through New Mexico. It forms the Texas-Mexican border, and, after a journey of 1,885 miles, empties into the Gulf of Mexico below Brownsville, Texas.

The major geographical features of the North American continent meet in Texas: seacoast, forest, mountains, desert, Great Plains. This towering pine near Beaumont, on the upper Gulf Coast, stands at the junction of coastal plain and southern pine forest. Beaumont is the site of the Spindletop Museum.

unimaginative it suggested that all the best ones had already been claimed by older cities, seemed like an overgrown version of Little Rock. Houston was still southern in flavor, still as redolent of magnolias as of oil, still a place where an occasional elderly gentleman might be seen in summertime wearing the traditional straw hat and white linen suit. Though it was the largest city in Texas, Houston had less than a million people. Its nascent cultural amenities did not outweigh the fearful heat and humidity — a climate so steamy the British consul was rumored to receive extra pay for service in a "hardship post." And while our university administrators periodically received earnest requests from foreigners for advice on the latest techniques in rice farming, the Rice Institute had nothing to do with agriculture but was instead the liberal arts-and-engineering legacy of a Yankee businessman named Rice who, like many others, had made a fortune in Texas in the freewheeling years after Reconstruction and, unlike most of them, left a substantial token of his gratitude before going back east to die. When I arrived, the Institute was less than fifty years old — a fair measure of the youth and immaturity of Texas, circa 1960.

Later, from Austin, I discovered the diversity of the Lone Star State. Exploring its 773-mile breadth from El Paso to Orange and its 801-mile length from the Panhandle to the Rio Grande's confluence with the Gulf of Mexico, I set foot in 221 of its 254 counties. In Texas the chief geographic features of the North American continent converge — the southern forests, the great plains, the tail end of the Rocky Mountains, the desert, the sea. Topographers divide the state into a half-dozen regions, economists divide it into several others; but all of these distinctions can be subsumed into one without doing violence to the truth. The signal division of Texas is between east and west. It follows a diagonal, northeast-to-southwest line which geologists call the Balcones Fault and motorists call Interstate 35. Eastward, Texas partakes of Dixie, though in parts that association has diminished almost to the point of invisibility; westward, Texas is first cousin to Arizona, New Mexico, and Colorado, the wide-open-spaces West. The classic Texas myth — the myth of cowboys and cattle and the open range — arose from the western side, but the realities of Texas power, political and economic, have always been securely fastened to the eastern side.

Statistics being the driest of sciences, statisticians delight in startling people with their more surprising findings, a thrill analogous to popping a paper bag in a sleepy classroom. First they lull their listeners: Texas, with 16 million cows, has more cattle than people; one in ten Texans has a pickup truck; 82 percent of Texas land consists of farms and ranches. Then, *bang!* they jolt them awake with the unexpected: 80 percent of Texans now live in cities. Today, Texas is overwhelmingly urban. It contains three of the country's ten largest cities: Houston, Dallas, San Antonio. Handmade cowboy boots are sported by men who have never touched a cow; the insides of high-speed elevators in downtown skyscrapers are lined with the finest leather.

Some of the most thoughtful Texas writers, among them the historian T. R. Fehrenbach and the novelist Larry McMurtry, now contend that the innermost truths of contemporary Texas are found in the cities, not on the ranches. Look there, they say, for the future of our literature. Without question, the rise of urban Texas has spawned a second Texas myth, parallel to the cowboy legend and arguably more powerful: the myth of the rich Texan, the wheeler-dealer, the oilman, the entrepreneur, the myth of absurd wealth and limitless possibility, a myth that finds its image and embodiment in Dallas.

But despite the state's reputation as a fountainhead of prosperity, the truth is that its per capita income remained *below* the national average until five years ago. In this respect as in many others, Texas since 1960 is a place transformed. The dominant feature I first noticed on Houston's skyline, the Texas National Bank, is now lost in a cluster of modern megaliths, and the once-shadowy silhouette of Dallas asserts itself in lights. Paul Burka, the political editor of *Texas Monthly,* measures the distance Texas has traveled by noting that as recently as fifteen years ago at least one of the three top restaurants in every major Texas city was a steak house, priding itself on "stuffed" baked potatoes, green goddess dressing, and little loaves of homemade bread; by the end of the 1970s, Houston and Dallas restaurants flaunted the latest chic trends in cuisine and often won national respect for their endeavors. Paying an ultimate compliment, Manhattan restaurateur Uncle Tai moved his four-star Chinese quarters lock, stock, and wok to Houston's dazzling Galleria area.

The rotunda of the Texas State Capitol is lined with native limestone. The 309-foot-high dome is made of copper.

A generation ago, Texas state government was a conservative Democratic stronghold, and its major cities were under the thumb of more-or-less benevolent oligarchies. Today, it is a two-party state by anyone's reckoning, and electoral reforms like single-member districts have put the oligarchs out to pasture. In 1960, the massive coastal development of Padre Island, the routine use of intrastate airlines instead of automobiles for travel between major cities, the influx of established corporate headquarters from the East Coast, even a mixed drink in a restaurant — all lay in the unimagined future. Within this generation, Texas shed its century-old colonial mentality, its immaturity, and its youth and became a cosmopolitan power to be reckoned with. Adding up the evidence, Burka concluded that the early seventies were "the dawn of modern Texas."

★

For most purposes, Texas history begins with the conquistadores. Pre-Columbian Texas has almost wholly vanished, leaving behind a few spellbinding cave paintings — works of such otherworldly mysteriousness that one aches to fathom the mind of those who drew them — and inexhaustible troves of broken pottery, *manos,* and *metates,* which excite archaeologists but few others. When the white man's civilization and the red man's ways proved irreconcilable, Texas slew its Indians, drove them out, or (on occasion) bought them out. In sharp contrast to other southwestern states, it numbers only two small Indian reservations: the Tiguas in El Paso and the Alabama-Coushatta near Woodville.

Had Texas lost its War of Independence, the landmarks of its Spanish past would be vested with greater significance. El Paso, San Antonio, Nacogdoches, even the little village of Presidio were all changed mightily by the Anglo-American migrations that sealed Texas to the United States, obscuring though not eclipsing their previous importance as centers of Spanish rule. Because Sam Houston and his followers won the War, we see the history of Texas through American eyes, not Mexican; we interpret its meaning through English sensibilities, not Spanish. Thus Nacogdoches, forty-five miles west of the Louisiana line, is remembered less for the Catholic mission founded there in 1716 than for serving in the following century as a major gateway for Anglo-American

settlers. Likewise, San Augustine: its old Spanish legacy yields pride of place to its claim as the "cradle of Texas." In Texas lore, the footsteps of Davy Crockett count for more than the benedictions of a hundred cassocked friars.

East Texas is a landscape of pine forests, hardwood bottomlands, red-earth farms, and cypress-fringed lakes. At the beginnings of the Texan consciousness, this *was* Texas. As a child I was taught that when the first Europeans reached America, the continent's eastern half was so densely forested that a squirrel could leap branch to branch from the Atlantic to the Mississippi without scuffing his feet on solid ground. Had he been able to swim the Great River, he could have continued his treetop journey all the way to East Texas before the woods ran out. The lesson, for those who want to understand the mental terrain of the pioneer Texans, is this: as southerners edging frontierward, they came from these woodlands and hewed to familiar surroundings.

A drive through East Texas today tells us something about them. The names of their towns — Palestine, Providence, Liberty Grove, Concord — speak of an older, different Texas, reflecting concerns which do not manifest themselves in twentieth century municipal nomenclature. One wonders why: are they things we take for granted or that we no longer care about? Southernness is woven into the texture of this region. Palestine, an old railroad town, would not seem strange to a visitor passing through from Alabama; along the route to Lufkin, the clear shallow streams, their exposed roots and vines, their mosses and ferns, could make a Virginian think of home. Hidden in tall grasses fifty yards from the highway, the Bobbitt Cemetery is indistinguishable from thousands of its kind scattered across the rural South. Many of the headstones are mere flat rocks, hand-carved with names and dates, some with the "Ns" cut backwards. A few miles away in Weches, a bright Confederate battle flag flies in a front yard, affixed to a pole fastened to a pine tree. The flag, common a generation ago, is now a rarity except on eighteen-wheelers and stock car racers, where its meaning is not always benign.

Fortune smiled unevenly on East Texas. Once this was cotton country. In some counties, farmers still scratch a living from less than fecund land. Their latest irritant is the fire ant, a newcomer whose nests can be seen along the right-of-way, usually squashed by the tracks of

The Fort Worth Stockyards, today a tourist attraction, contains hatters, bootmakers, and vendors of custom western gear.

swerving pickup trucks driven by farmhands determined to even the score. In the region around Tyler, Kilgore, and Longview, however, what matters is what lies under the earth, not what can be grown on it. The East Texas Oil Field was the largest known pool of oil in the world when it was discovered by wildcatter C. M. "Dad" Joiner in 1930. Until modern technology simplified the drilling process, this part of Texas was crammed with derricks—more than a thousand within the city limits of Kilgore alone. Fortunes were made or missed depending on the lay of one's land (and, sometimes, on the proclivity of one's neighbors to drill slant-holes). The lucky ones rose from impoverished homesteaders to landed gentry overnight. Tyler, the City of Roses, is today a kind of mini-Dallas, its southern sweetness interfused with the scent of prosperity beyond the imagining of the rough-hewn folk who first trekked to Texas.

At the other end of East Texas, past the great pine plantations of the lumber lords, past the huge reservoirs like Sam Rayburn and Toledo Bend that have transformed small-town life, bringing lake recreation and a glimpse of the open sky to woodland dwellers—beyond all this lies the Big Thicket, a secluded, secret corner still in parts pristine. Its deep hardwood forests are like nothing else in Texas, a haven for wildlife and rare plants from four biological regions. In a compromise between loggers and environmentalists, isolated sections of the Thicket are being set aside for inclusion in Big Thicket National Preserve. There, visitors following trails through the dense foliage can search for a glimpse of rare orchids and listen hopefully for the sound of the— perhaps extinct—ivory-billed woodpecker.

★

The southeast Texas industrial triangle of Beaumont, Port Arthur, and Orange receives fifty to fifty-nine inches of rain a year—more than soggy New Orleans. Houston logs in at a little less, forty-eight, but that suffices to sustain a hothouse climate which cast an enervating pall until air conditioning brought liberation in the 1950s. In the jargon of city planners, Houston is a "low-density spread city." In this it is not alone. Austin, San Antonio, El Paso, and the rest are creatures of the automobile age too. Dallas covers more than 375 square miles (almost four times the area of St. Louis), and Houston is bigger

yet. The featureless expanse of coastal plains placed no physical obstacle in the path of Houston's pell-mell growth. It lacks the dominant landmarks, the ocean and mountains, that give orientation to Los Angeles. Many of its thoroughfares follow the same unpredictable diagonals down which they were laid long ago as rural roads, relieving Houston from the relentless gridlike regularity of sunbelt cities like Phoenix, but multiplying one's chances of getting lost in the sprawl.

Houston's skyline is the city's equivalent of the mountains it does not have. It is almost as if, with nothing of nature to be awed by, man decided to awe himself with his own works, to build his own mountains. Pennzoil, Exxon, Shell—the downtown district is a High Sierra of corporate towers. Some boast a hoary Texan lineage; others are newly relocated from the East, bringing thousands of transplanted employees with such decidedly unTexan tastes and sensibilities as opera, sailboats, and pastrami. Its population nearing two million, Houston has come a long way from the rambunctious days when it was called a "whiskey and trombone town."

For a time, as the center of the nation's petrochemical industry, Houston rode the crest of the oil boom. The good times appeared unending; the freeways bulged with cars bearing Michigan license plates and rust-belt refugees. But when the price of oil plummented in 1982, Houston's one-note petroleum economy suffered badly, and for the first time Houstonians gazed with a twinge of envy at the burgeoning high-tech centers of Austin and Dallas. Even at its giddiest economic heights, Houston does not easily win the hearts of visitors. It has its beauties—the stately residences of River Oaks, the massive live oaks that line South Main. It has its glitter—the luxurious, multi-tiered shopping malls, the ice rinks. But there are other parts, miles of them, where prosperity seems never to have touched.

On a clear day, though, venture out and see the essential Houston. Everyone who knows this undeniably vital city has his own idiosyncratic list, often at odds with the cautious recommendations (Fine Arts Museum, Space Center, Zoo), proffered by the tourist office. Look first at the downtown city hall, knee high to corporate skyscrapers, a dwarf among giants, the perfect metaphor, a Texas politician once told me, for the historic relationship between business and government in the Lone Star State. Drive through the Montrose district, formerly

Alligator juniper, named for its rough bark, occurs in the Hill Country and West Texas in protected canyons.

a neighborhood of exemplary, brick, middle-class homes, now a chaotic jumble of apartments, restaurants, and every sort of commercial enterprise imaginable — the vivid consequence of Houston's total lack of zoning laws. Pause at the Rothko Chapel, a somber half-lit room lined with the last bleak works of American painter Mark Rothko. Soothing to some, disquieting to others, this gift of the DeMenil family is arguably the single greatest work of art in Texas.

Look at the wayward flying saucer, the Astrodome, Houston's number one gee-whiz sight. When the plans for this air-conditioned stadium were announced more than twenty years ago, nothing comparable had ever been built. Houstonians naturally visualized something capped with a single translucent plastic bubble. Instead the dome consisted of a ceiling made from hundreds of separate panes beneath which grass was expected to grow. It did — until the panes were painted over to placate outfielders who claimed they lost fly balls in the glare. The *ad hoc* solution: Astroturf, an artificial grass that quickly became more popular than the real thing. At outdoor arenas across America, college administrators began scraping up the well-trimmed playing fields and replacing them with synthetic turf at costs exceeding half a million dollars per field. Necessity, as Texas entrepreneurs routinely prove, is indeed the mother of invention.

And last, ponder the "why" of Houston: the fifty-mile-long Ship Channel, best viewed from an overlook beside the Turning Basin. This man-made waterway let oceangoing freighters bypass little Galveston, Houston's aristocratic senior on an island in the Gulf, and transformed the upstart Bayou City into America's third-largest port.

Some places in Texas do not comport with the Texas myth. Galveston is one of these. In the nineteenth century it was a celebrated city, wealthy and proud, a showcase of Victorian style in largely barbarous surroundings. On its shores arrived the European immigrants who, for various reasons, chose to try their luck in the raw southwest instead of the tenements of New York. Years ago, I crossed paths with one, a white-haired old man tending a roadside honey stand in the little central Texas town of Gause. His name was Wilhelm Piefer, "the Bee Man." At thirteen, he had landed penniless in Galveston on a ship from Germany. The vagaries of fortune

brought him to Gause and taught him about bees. Well into his eighties, his eyes still brightened at the mention of Galveston, at the excitement and the drama which had enveloped him there so long ago.

Galveston is still proud, but no longer is it wealthy or celebrated. Its finery was swept away in a cataclysmic hurricane on September 8, 1900, that killed more than six thousand people in the single greatest natural disaster in American experience. A seawall now protects the city, the old Strand district is artfully restored, and ample beaches draw crowds of sunbathers in the summer, but Galveston is a backwater, an odd relic of a vanished Texas, dwindling toward an uncertain future. It is the only major Texas city whose population has declined in the past twenty years.

Economists with a penchant for geometry call the Texas Gulf Coast "the Industrial Crescent." Crescent-shaped it is, but long stretches are anything but industrial. Sandy formations known as barrier islands shelter the mainland from the Gulf waters proper, creating bays and estuaries that provide ideal breeding grounds for marine life. Commercial fisheries are big business in the Texas Gulf ports, but ironically shrimp, not a fish at all, provides 99 percent of their total annual gross profits.

The Gulf Coast is an acquired taste. Flat, humid, and cluttered by the debris from shipping and offshore oil rigs, it is not everyone's idea of maritime beauty. It is best where it is wild: the largely roadless national seashore of Padre Island and serenely isolated Matagorda Island. Recently incorporated into the Texas park system as a wildlife refuge and accessible only by air or boat, Matagorda is a favorite winter destination for the endangered whooping crane.

In February, 1985, a different sort of gathering took place on Matagorda, one which illustrates the special state of mind that makes Texas such a distinctive place. Two dozen of the state's highest officials took leave of their duties and repaired to the island for an overnight stay, camping under the stars in commemoration of a historic moment in the state's past. The occasion was the 300-year anniversary of the French explorer LaSalle's first landfall on the Texas coast. The fleur-de-lis of the French kings was raised on a flagpole atop a dune and the exploits of LaSalle were duly recalled before the gathering adjourned to the quiet camaraderie of the campfire. Similar unpublicized retreats were held in

Vast tank farms containing imported crude oil surround the chemical refineries of the Port of Freeport, south of Houston.

1981, at an obscure West Texas ranch where the state's last Indian battle occurred exactly a century before, and again in 1983, at a remote desert site where the final silver spike of the Southern Pacific Railroad joined Texas to the Pacific in 1883. In Texas, history is remembered in and out of school.

A pleasant, gull-flecked bay city with a congenial air, Corpus Christi is the urban center of the South Texas coast. Holiday-makers have turned nearby North Padre Island into a boomland of vacation condominiums despite the dire warnings of weather-minded folk who compute roulette-wheel odds on hurricanes along this low shore and remember the fifteen-foot storm surge that obliterated Galveston.

Hurricanes in the Gulf, like earthquakes in California, are inevitable: the only question is when. Perhaps that is why the sparkling Art Museum of South Texas on Corpus Christi's waterfront has but a single window opening to the sea. But I like to think there is a different reason. From that window one sees only the steady undulations of the water, a sight of astonishing beauty, especially at dusk. If, as some say, the sea is as close as mortal man can be to infinity, the effect of that window is awesome and intimidating. Situated among the artworks as though it were one of them, set in a frame of its own, it becomes a painting-in-action. Just outside these walls, it seems to say, beyond the color and life and human creativity surrounding us, monochromatic infinity patiently waits. It is the South Texas answer to the Rothko Chapel.

★

Twenty years ago, for reasons that still chill the memory, Dallas was as "out" a city as any in America; today it is suddenly the "in" place to be. Even the critics who kicked Dallas when it was down have kind words to say. People who insisted it was the last place in Texas they'd want to live are talking about "upscale amenities" and "The City That Works." Is it the money-conscious eighties? Dallas must be doing something right.

You do not have to prefer *The Wall Street Journal* to *Rolling Stone* to love Dallas, but it helps. Money is the measure of accomplishment, the way Dallas keeps score. Transplanted New York writer Peter Applebome has studied the place for years with the same affectionate wonder Margaret Mead brought to the South Sea

Islanders, and in his mind there is no doubt: "Success is really the only game to play in Dallas. If you don't play it, you're nothing." By the same token, if you play it well, the sky's the limit. H. Ross Perot, the former IBM employee from Texarkana, became one of the city's most influential citizens after he turned his ideas into a billion-dollar enterprise called Electronic Data Systems, Inc. What is the goal of life? "To be indomitable, to be joyous," say the Greeks. "Success," says Dallas.

Entrepreneurs are the heroes of such a place, and work is therapeutic. I once asked worldwide real estate magnate Trammell Crow about the unusual paintings on the wall of his Dallas office. Did he, I wondered, have a passion for art? "Yugoslavian naives," he replied ebulliently. "They're not a particular interest of mine. I just *bought* some. I have no passions—except work. And my family." Perot, a crew-cut ex-Navy man, put it this way: "People who spend their lifetimes searching for pleasure don't find it. You know, there's a lot of pleasure in leading a full, active, working life, with a little bit of time for fun. But when fun becomes your life, it doesn't work."

Perot's ideas on education are beginning to have a profound impact. As chairman of the governor's Select Committee on Public Education, he stumped the state for no-nonsense, back-to-basics reforms, and the legislature, meeting in special session, enacted many of them into law. Extracurricular activities that took time away from academic achievement were a special target.

The committee's appeals made high-flying Texans look soberly at their state's long-range future. "Historically," Perot observed, "Texas has had a large landmass and a small population. Our landmass is constant. Our population is growing rapidly. We're running out of oil and gas. Our children are going to have to live by their brains and wits. They're going to have to compete and *win* in international competition. You don't get a second-place prize in business. No red ribbons."

Nowhere in Texas is the blue-ribbon spirit more pervasive than Dallas. A city with no special reason to be, it has survived and prospered by believing in itself. Its residents affectionately call it "D" ("Big D" is tourist talk, like "Frisco"), and it seems to have extruded right out of the north Texas prairie in an astonishing collective act of will.

Dallas has a sleekness Houston lacks. It possesses all the accoutrements of any big American city — tall

The spring Azalea Festival begins the season for Tyler where half the field-grown roses in the United States are produced.

buildings, industrial sections, magnificent homes, Vietnamese immigrants, gentrification, art museums, rush-hour traffic. What makes it distinctive is the proportions: Dallas is the nirvana of mainstream, middle-class America — and *that,* despite the tribulations of the city's impoverished, heavily black south side, is what Dallas is all about. Just as no one goes to San Francisco for the Sunset district, or to New York for the Bronx, people find the quintessential D in sprawling, affluent North Dallas. Here even the Eastern Orthodox Church of Saints Constantine and Helen is located on a street named Betty Jane Lane.

The consumer paradise of North Dallas, a land of mega-malls, is connected to downtown by the Dallas North Tollway. Dallas is the only city in Texas with a toll road — and, I have often suspected, the only Texas city that would tolerate one. Some of the northern suburbs — Plano, Richardson — comprise the high-tech territory Texans call Silicon Prairie. Jack Kilby, a self-effacing, six-foot-six Dallas inventor, may be the man most responsible for its existence. Working as an engineer at Texas Instruments, he came up with the idea of the silicon chip on July 24, 1958. His insight transformed the real estate values of North Dallas and the way the world does business. A couple of years ago, I went by to visit him at his inventor's den in a nondescript Dallas office building. Dressed in a flannel shirt and gray slacks, chain smoking Carltons, he was trying to teach himself word processing on a Texas Instruments computer. "I only got it last week," said the man who made the whole thing possible. "I wasn't aware I needed one."

Most North Dallas suburbs forbid the sale of alcohol, but 242 voters were enough to convert the tiny village of Addison into a two-mile-square oasis. Now its main street is packed with restaurants and singles bars, and the city is rich with the revenue from liquor taxes. The police drive Volvos; the building that once housed Addison's old schoolhouse is a nightclub called The Magic Time Machine. It is a young suburban world where grandmothers and babysitters are equally hard to find.

Basic to the Dallas civic character is an endearing sort of earnestness. It is a self-satisfied city with much to be satisfied about. But by taking itself so seriously it affords an irresistible target for anyone who enjoys puncturing the complacency of others. "Do It For Dallas" is the motto of every noble public endeavor, every volunteer's

Good Works. The esprit produces broad-based committee tomes like *Goals for Dallas* and catalogues of municipal accomplishment like *Dallas Innovations, 1980-81,* a roster of mastered problems so meticulous that even the Dog Registration Improvement Program did not escape notice. After methodically classifying charitable giving into "the arts" and "the diseases," Dallas philanthropists drive for victory in both. "My disease is cystic fibrosis," a young socialite told me, referring not to her physical condition but to the object of her bounty.

Like the Swiss, Dallas makes a virtue of orderliness. *Rules are rules* is the city's ethos; rules exist for the good of us all, and they *will* be enforced. On the whole, this helps make Dallas a notably pleasant place to live—city services are efficient, and the other guy obeys the traffic laws too. But the impulse to regiment is always there, twitching under the surface. Molly Ivins, a liberal writer who has kept her sense of humor amid the city's idiosyncrasies, tells of the time police shot a man who was jaywalking. "But he was armed," she protests. "Dallas has *never* shot an *unarmed* jaywalker."

Turtle Creek in Highland Park is one of the loveliest green spaces anywhere, but picnics, messy things, are *strenglich verboten.* A walled park called Thanks-Giving Square in the center of downtown contains not a single bench or seat, and to discourage vagrants its landscaped grounds are closed and locked more often than they are open. Walls, in fact, are one of D's distinguishing features. The Art Museum's new sculpture garden is an outright festival of walls. At the growing edge of far North Dallas, walled clumps of townhouses rise amid acres of yet undeveloped prairie like medieval fortress-villages on the Pomeranian plain. Enclosed spaces sometimes are considered more real than the unenclosed. Fenced and guarded Cottonwood Valley, part of a sophisticated, security-conscious new suburb called Las Colinas, is advertised to buyers as a spot "where the privacy of the countryside is preserved."

Not surprisingly for a place that thinks countryside started out private, Dallas recoils at being thought a western city. Its businessmen would sooner be exiled to Minsk than be caught wearing cowboy boots with their three-piece suits, and computer stores outnumber barbecue places three to one. For reassurance, Dallas has traditionally looked east. "They really want the Yankees to love 'em," said one Dallasite, himself a former

The 66,000 seats in Houston's 208-foot-tall Astrodome are color-coded by ticket price in the upper sections.

Yankee. The habit is paradoxical but persistent. "Dallas doesn't realize it doesn't share the *values* of the East at all," says author Prudence Mackintosh, a Highland Park mother. "That's not who we are, or how we live." But in Dallas eyes, a word of praise from east of the Hudson outweighs the approbation of fellow Texans.

In the end, it is attitude that makes Dallas different. Dallasites look at the glittering lights of downtown from the Woodall Rogers Freeway on a winter evening—lots of people are still working hard, though the sky has long been dark—and they see Manhattan on the prairie. They remember Sherman or Denton or Waco, any of the lesser towns, and think: all this is here because our forebears *willed* it here, and now the responsibility for moving it along is ours. At bottom, I suspect, is an unspoken amazement that D exists at all. *All of us have to keep pushing, keep believing,* says the Doer for Dallas, *because if we don't, we'll wake up one morning and discover it was all a dream.* The city will de-extrude back into the prairie, leaving nothing but waving grama grass and a hawk circling in the sky, vanished like Brigadoon.

★

"Twin cities" usually have little of the twin about them —one thinks of staid St. Paul and toney Minneapolis— and the two unequal halves of the "Dallas-Fort Worth Metroplex" are no exception. A visitor arriving at DFW Airport who collects his bags and heads westward will be deposited in a very different sort of place than Dallas.

Even the name "Dallas-Fort Worth" grates exquisitely upon the nerves of residents in the state's fourth largest city. Fort Worth and Dallas grew up independently, born of different needs. They served, and still serve, different hinterlands and have come together only as a consequence of prosperity. Thirty years ago, they were such reluctant bedfellows that the first attempt to replace Love Field with a regional airport closer to Fort Worth failed ignominiously when Dallasites boycotted the new facility because the terminal's doors faced west. Since then the two cities have realized that theirs is a marriage of convenience without possibility of divorce.

In the thirty-two miles from Dallas to Fort Worth the elevation rises 158 feet, beginning a steady change in both landscape and life-style that carries across the rest of Texas. The conventional wisdom says that Fort Worth is Cowtown, the big city of cattle and railroads and western ways, Texan to its core, everything Dallas is not. Despite the aerospace industry, a water garden designed by Philip Johnson, the most gratifying art museum in Texas (the Kimbell), and a burst of downtown construction which belatedly has given Fort Worth a skyline of its own, the conventional wisdom remains largely true. Main Street is still paved with red brick. A place called Billy Bob's Texas is still the world's largest country-and-western honky-tonk. The Amon Carter Museum of Western Art is a waterhole for those who prefer Remingtons and Russells to old masters. The stockyards, cattle-less in this age of feedlots, have been preserved, and anybody can walk right up the street and buy a pair of handmade boots. You can still get roaring drunk and start an honest brawl on the Jacksboro Highway any Saturday night. You can go from home to work without tithing the toll bucket, and nobody really cares whether you drive a Mercedes or a Ford. In the Texan psyche, Fort Worth is still the Faithful Son, true to the state's soul. *When you're with him in Dallas,* goes the lovesick refrain of a popular song, *does Fort Worth ever cross your mind?* Texans believe that as long as Fort Worth is there, when they tire of chasing after false gods they can still come home.

★

Vast ranchlands roll westward, ever drier, beyond Fort Worth. Except in the eyes of those who were born there —and over a six-pack or two, some of them have been known to confide their doubts—it is a landscape devoid of beauty. Most of its magic resides in the town names themselves, resonant with cowboy legend: Wichita Falls, Abilene, San Angelo. One thinks of the expression British settlers invented to convey their mixture of frustration and respect for the endless undeveloped sameness of the highlands of East Africa: *M.M.B.A.,* they said, "Miles and Miles of Bloody Africa." Driving west from Fort Worth — northwest, due west, southwest, it doesn't matter which — you are swallowed up by such distances. *M.M.B.T.*

A fifty-five m.p.h. speed limit is an absurdity where time is money and a day's work may cover hundreds of miles. Ranchers are not literary men, but one offered me a copy of T. R. Fehrenbach's history of Texas, *Lone Star,*

To the people of the ranching country west of Fort Worth, raising horses is still a serious business.

which puts the idea most succinctly: "The law did not understand certain realities in the West, almost certainly because the lawmakers and enforcers, all men of the regions farther east, did not understand them. …Logic was only logic in the West if it visibly worked." When, in the 1940s, a federal official came to Texas to persuade the governor to endorse the wartime thirty-five m.p.h. speed limit, which was voluntary, the chief executive listened patiently to the young man's cogent reasons and after a thoughtful pause replied, "Son, if you drive thirty-five miles an hour in *Texas,* you don't ever *arrive!"*

Out there in M.M.B.T., the contrast between eastern rules and local practice can be sharp. Controlled access on the interstate means nothing to a rancher in a four-wheel-drive vehicle who reaches his gate miles before he reaches the appropriate off-ramp. Not surprisingly, he cuts right on across. Catalytic converters are apt to set fire to precious grass, so gas tanks are hammered open to permit the use of leaded gasoline, ecologists be damned. In West Texas, one glimpses the great swirling public issues dimly, like a storm at sea seen from dry land. But laws drafted by authorities far away in Washington or Austin eventually arrive on the rancher's doorstep, packaged and obligatory.

As the traveler drives westward, the places Larry McMurtry wrote about in *The Last Picture Show* give way to the High Plains around Amarillo, a treeless terrain of such extraordinary flatness that Spanish explorers who wandered there in search of the fabled Seven Cities of Gold drove stakes in the ground to mark their path. Amarillo is still cattle kingdom; its urban rival, Lubbock, some two hours away on what is known as the South Plains, is the heartland of a farm economy thriving on water pumped from the rapidly depleting Ogallala Aquifer. Texas has been the number-one cotton-producing state since 1880, and, astonishingly, with the advent of irrigation, the bulk of it has come from these plains, not the old plantation counties back east.

Amarillo has a relaxed air. I once knew a lovely young woman of German extraction whose family ranch just outside town had cold beer on tap in the barn; no one thought it particularly strange. By contrast, an organized antipathy to alcohol made Lubbock until recently the largest "dry" city in the English-speaking world. Amarillo is probably the only Texas municipality of its size, 150,000, that still revolves around a downtown

cafe, opening before dawn, where everyone from rancher to judge meets over coffee and homemade sourdough biscuits. It also has its resident millionaire eccentric, a gentleman named Stanley Marsh 3 who achieved celebrity status by burying a row of ten Cadillacs nose-down, fins-up, alongside Interstate 40, a gesture immediately recognized as a Statement in national art circles. The Cadillacs are still there—slowly disappearing under the midnight depredations of other vintage car owners in need of the occasional spare part. Unmentioned in the Texas Tourist Bureau's official *Travel Handbook,* Marsh's Cadillacs have nevertheless become the number one word-of-mouth attraction for bored travelers crossing the Panhandle.

Texas produces 29 percent of America's oil and 34 percent of its natural gas, giving the state first rank in both. South of Lubbock, in the Permian Basin, a pair of rival cities dominate the modern-day Texas Oil Patch. The transformation wrought upon Midland and Odessa by the 1923 discovery of oil on impoverished, overgrazed ranchland can be measured by the census reports for Odessa's county, Ector: between 1920 and 1960 population doubled, tripled, or quadrupled every ten years.

Unlike the East Texas Field, the Permian Basin is a collection of isolated pools, not a vast black underground lake. The most fabulous pool is the Yates field at Iraan, one of the richest reserves on earth, and so shallow that its treasures can be pumped out by hydrostatic pressure from the water table. The proverbial stick-a-pencil-in-the-ground-and-get-splattered-by-the-black-stuff story made Ira Yates, the grocer on whose land the first strike came, a very rich man. The crude oil already produced there, if refined into gasoline, could propel 3½ million motorcycles around the world at the equator, with enough left over to operate 2000 lawnmowers continuously since the time of Christ. And geologists say more than half is still underground.

Now it is firmly in the hands of corporations. The oil flows invisibly eastward in the great pipelines—at $30 a barrel, $3.75 million of oil a day. But, except for a splendid public school, you would be hard-pressed to find a trace of this sensational wealth in the tough little town of Iraan, population 1358. When I visited late one October, the air was heavy with the stench of hydrogen sulfide gas. Young men roamed the main street pelting

The Intracoastal Waterway provides protected passage for commercial barges and small boats the entire length of the Texas coast.

cars with water balloons, celebrating Halloween before dark, clearly in the mainstream of American mischief. "The rich strike, the big bonanza," wrote Bernard de Voto, "is only half the story. ... The collapse of the boom is the very essence of the Western experience." I thought of the abandoned mining towns in the far West, their ghostly remains, and wondered what would become of Iraan when the last drop of oil was gone.

In the three thousand-foot-plus altitudes of this region, as well as in the Panhandle, wine grapes may be the wave of the future. Nights are cool enough to help them strike the indispensable balance between sweetness and acidity. Surprisingly, for Texas seldom resembles California's Napa Valley, European varietals have been cultivated with encouraging results by the University of Texas and other growers, using a drip irrigation system that conserves water. The state's populist Agriculture Commissioner, Jim Hightower, has declared that wine will be "the next big thing from Texas." If so, it would be an economic boon for parts of the state living a marginal existence. Its very presence symbolizes the changes that have taken place since the Comanche horsemen ruled the plains scarcely a century ago. "Wine is a part of the soul of Europe," wrote the Englishman Hilaire Belloc. "When we find it in far-off places, it is but a colony of ourselves."

★

Austin is every Texan's favorite city. None has changed as much in the past twenty years. When I arrived in 1966, it was a casual place, a university and state government town and not much more. The description "laid-back," which residents still invoke, was apt then: you could take a bottle of bourbon in a brown bag to the Split Rail Inn and hear Kenneth Threadgill and the Hootenanny Hoots sing old Jimmie Rodgers songs every Saturday and Sunday night, or you could prop your feet up on the back porch railing of Mary's Dry Creek Inn and watch the sun set over cedar-covered hills. The Split Rail burned down years ago, and today developers are plowing up those hills.

The world found out about Austin in the 1970s. Perhaps it was country music fever and the TV show called *Austin City Limits*. Since then, the Texas capital has doubled in size. It is a high-tech, fast-money town, the

sort of place where real estate prices knock you on your ear. But for all that, blessedly, it keeps a flavor all its own: genial, tolerant, whimsical, outdoorsy. And not even real estate developers can take away its setting.

Willie Morris once wrote that Austin is "the place where the South ends." The phrase was a good one. On one side of the city lie the black-earth prairies that are kin to most of America between Austin and the Potomac. On the other rises the hardscrabble Hill Country, beloved of Lyndon Johnson and described masterfully by Robert Caro in his biography of LBJ. "The trap," Caro called it: a land of bewitching vistas, interlaced with spring-fed streams, near-impossible to wrest a living from. This is the German part of Texas, Republican and Unionist in the Civil War. In towns like Fredericksburg and New Braunfels, German still occasionally is heard.

Pre-eminent among the state's 155 colleges and universities, the University of Texas at Austin is wealthy beyond measure with oil and gas royalties from wells drilled on state lands. Its $2 billion dollar endowment is second only to Harvard's, and its $4 an hour tuition is the lowest in the country. But its century-old constitutional directive to become "a University of the first class"— had proved problematical.

For long years the University wavered in its purpose, uncertain whether to explore knowledge for the sake of knowledge, or to train young Texans for vocations in a corporate economy. Now, the University's efforts have begun to bear impressive fruit: a Humanities Research Center with literary treasures that are the envy of scholars around the world; $15 million in newly endowed professorial chairs; and millions more for research funds and equipment to help the next generation of Texans.

★

San Antonio is the tenth largest city in the United States and the only one with a Mexican-American majority. With its Spanish colonial architecture and its meandering River Walk, it has a visual charm no other Texas city can match. It also is home to the Institute of Texan Cultures, a museum which portrays the ethnic history of Texas in riveting detail. For a long time San Antonio rested, not only on its laurels as the Alamo City, but on a military-base economy that was recession-proof. Today San Antonio is no longer the sleepy city it

Twenty years of labor by Indians and Spanish missionaries completed San Antonio's stone Mission Concepcion in 1755.

was ten years ago, or even five; it has gone high-tech. Many consider it the most exciting city in the state.

I spent a week as a guest of the Jesuit Fathers of Nuestra Señora de Guadalupe, a typical church on San Antonio's West Side *barrio,* living in a tiny room and venturing out to learn as much as I could about the sprawling community around me. In contrast to suburban churches, Guadalupe was abuzz with activity throughout the day, a social center for thousands of Catholics within its mile-square parish. There were basketball games, meals for the elderly, mariachi practice, and daily masses, commonly in Spanish.

But no feature of the church received more attention than a little statue that stood in an outdoor chapel outside my window. It depicted a suffering Christ, in agony under a crown of thorns. Beside it two bulletin boards were pinned with prayers. At dusk each day, a steady stream of battered old cars, pickup trucks, and vans arrived one by one, discharging parishioners who shyly slipped back along the narrow passageway to the chapel and added a photograph of a loved one or a note of supplication to the crowded boards. Feeling like an intruder, I read one message. "Dear Lord," it said in a shaky hand, "and our heavenly father, please help me on life and please sent my beloved wife back to me. Once we're together help us live the life you want us to live. Also please help me find a job. Love you. — HDE."

Across El Paso Street, Dolores Solis makes tortillas twice a day and sells them hot, just as she has for eighteen years. The west side is dotted with such individually owned shops. Captivated by the aromas, I came into her factory and asked to be instructed. She was delighted to oblige.

"We soak the corn the day before," she said. "White corn, in some water, with some lime. We cook it about two hours" — I watched as one of her helpers stirred the brew with a little wooden oar — "and then we leave it in *reposo* all night. You know why. Because it swallows the water. Then we mash it, and take away the lime, and drain it in the *molino,* and it comes out *masa* !" With the bold gesture of a virtuoso magician, she scooped up a handful of the grainy Indian cornmeal and plopped it on the rollers of a tortilla machine. The machine took it from there — flattening it to a thin sheet, cutting it into circles, rolling them down a conveyor belt where they toasted and tumbled into a waiting basket.

Mrs. Solis patted the machine. "It has a stainless steel cover," she said, "but we don't use it, because we like to see the tortillas coming along." She held up a lightly-browned example of her art, measuring its plumpness with fingers like calipers. "There is more profit where the tortilla is thinner," she said. "If you go to those big factories — so many, so thin. But we make ours thick, like they should be. We are doing fine. We are making right now about fifty dollars a day."

★

South of San Antonio, Texas does not yield its secrets readily. This is the home of vast cattle empires like the King Ranch, closed societies shielded from an outsider's idle curiosity. Until a few decades ago, even federal highways did not cross these lands. Kenedy County still seems more a private preserve than part of Texas; travelers passing through cannot stop for gasoline.

After this monotonous chapparal country, the sudden sight of plowed green land, palm trees, and grapefruit orchards comes as a surprise. Hidalgo County in the Lower Rio Grande Valley is the most productive agricultural county in Texas and among the most productive anywhere in America.

The Valley, as Texans call it, is a strange blend of wealth and penury, of America and Mexico. In winter, retired folk arrive to savor its mild climate, infusing the economy with seasonal cash. Its alluvial soil supports thriving vegetable farms. There is money to be made in the Valley, but there is also savage poverty, and it is at its worst in the no-man's-land of the *colonias.*

I roamed about these places, which often lack electricity and running water, in the company of a memorable Mexican-American leader named Leo J. Leo, a grocer whose store dominated the little Valley town of LaJoya the way big Leo dominated a room.

"This was part of the Reynosa Viejo *ejido* grant of 1749," he said, pointing to an onion field. "This was the town common, and later on it became part of the United States. The Mexican people kept on living here, but they didn't have title — how could they? It belonged to the town. It wasn't until 1935 that they got a court to subdivide it. This piece here went to the lawyers." We drove down the rocky streets. He compared them to the Mexican town of Reynosa across the river. "The people who

Elaborate costume is as much a part of the charro *tradition in South Texas as is the Mexican* vaquero's *skill in the saddle.*

live here are all migrants, all Mexicans, every one of them. They've brought these blocks over and built these homes themselves."

Alone among the old Texas borderlands, the Valley is still contested. Mexican-Americans are the overwhelming majority, 70 to 80 percent and more; Anglo-Americans, with rare exceptions, still hold the banks, the agribusiness, the manufacturing. It is a delicate compromise, the sort of balance Middle Eastern diplomats once described as "the Levantine Solution": one group holds political power, the other, economic, in an uneasy truce. Many older Anglos view the future with mistrust. Deep down, they say, too many Mexicans divide their loyalties and look forward to the day when these hinterlands of the ancient Montezumas are reclaimed.

★

For centuries, puzzled explorers under various flags were convinced the Rio Grande should be navigable. The river was a known quantity at El Paso and again far downstream in the Lower Valley, but between these familiar landmarks it passed through a rugged, Indian-haunted wilderness the Spaniards called the *despoblado* —the unpopulated place. We now know the Rio Grande courses for much of this way through spectacular deep canyons, boulder-strewn and shallow except when sudden summer floods come crashing through. Canoes and rafts afford the only safe passage. But as late as 1850 the ill-starred Love Expedition was still trying to navigate upstream from Rio Grande City to El Paso in fifty-foot flat-bottomed boats, and it was not until 1899 that the river was finally mapped.

Since 1944 the Rio Grande's most scenic portions have been preserved within the boundaries of Big Bend National Park, and an even more remote 126-mile reach is part of the National Wild River System. The old *despoblado* now goes by the name of the Trans-Pecos. It is still the least-crowded region of Texas and the one most consonant with the Texas myth. In its customs, its manners, and the character of the independent souls who choose to live there, the Trans-Pecos is Texas as the world imagines it.

Considering that Texas has seventy-five years of frontier history and so many authentic heroes to its credit, it is odd that its single best-known personality is probably a grizzled old gunslinger of dubious repute named Judge Roy Bean. A barkeeper who followed the railroad crews with a portable saloon in the 1880s, Bean set up shop permanently at a little water stop called Langtry when the railroad work was done. Somehow—no one is sure just how—he wangled an official appointment as Justice of the Peace. And there, in the immense isolation west of the Pecos River canyon, ensconced on the porch of his Jersey Lilly Saloon, he *was* the law until the early twentieth century. Bean never hanged a man—his legend has become entangled with "Hanging Judge Parker" of Fort Smith, Arkansas, who assuredly did — but his judicial style was at best improvisatory.

At least one federal judge later concluded that Bean was the man for his time and place, his commonsense justice being all the rough community would tolerate. Not everyone agrees. Trans-Pecos rancher Pard Schupach remembered sitting down in what he called "Bean's joint" to order a glass of beer. "He looked over at me and said, 'Hey do you know I'm the Law West of the Pecos?' 'Well,' I said, 'Do you know I'm the law north, east, south, and west of the Pecos?' I was just a cowpuncher, but he thought I was a Texas Ranger." Schupach chuckled at his hoax. "I was in Langtry the day he died," he said. "He was a grand rascal, a criminal. Now you're young and you don't know what happened. You think Judge Roy was something to see. Most men despised the look of him."

It is uncertain what women thought. Bean's one true love, hopelessly unrequitable, was the disarmingly beautiful British actress Lillie Langtry, who, it is said, counted among her beaus England's Prince of Wales, later Edward VII. The judge sent her love letters and insisted the town had been named for her.

Bean's original saloon is preserved in a superb roadside museum called the Roy Bean Visitor Center, run by the Texas Highway Department. Manager Jack Skiles, a local rancher, is the official Keeper of the Beanish Flame. One afternoon, he took a sabbatical and showed me the interesting country around Langtry. We poked through hollowed-out Indian caves, where blackened ceilings and piles of flat rocks used for cooking remained just as they were millennia ago. Stacks of chewed quids lay among the ash. The long-vanished Indians led an arduous existence. "Don't you know they were tough!" Skiles mused. "They'd eat grasshoppers,

At the LBJ Space Center near Houston, visitors can see moon rocks, a full-scale Skylab, and spacecraft that have traveled to the moon.

rats, whatever they could find." At a "buffalo drop," a cliff over which the Indians stampeded animals to their deaths, piles of buffalo bones lay where archaeologists had excavated them. Carbon-dating proved the ruse had worked for thousands of years. Not far away was the campsite of oriental laborers who built the railroad in 1883. There, perfectly preserved in the dry air, were Chinese coins, broken woks, and opium tins.

Lillie Langtry finally came to town in 1904, fulfilling Roy Bean's fondest dreams. But the whiskery old judge had, alas, keeled over and died in his saloon ten months before. The townspeople presented her with his pistol, which still sits in her museum on the Isle of Jersey, and she rode off to California, never to return.

★

Most of the Trans-Pecos is young country, barely a hundred years settled. History is biography there—what one's own kinfolk, or one's neighbor's kinfolk, did. Sometimes the eyewitnesses are still among us, leading quiet, unexceptional lives, the repositories of astonishing memories.

Lela Weatherby, a retired teacher in the little town of Fort Davis, spent decades instructing pupils in the proper conjugation of Latin verbs and the intricacies of Caesar's *Commentaries,* but long before that, on Christmas morning, 1917, at the ranch of Lucas Brite, she found herself in the midst of a raid by followers of the Mexican rebel Pancho Villa. In the dimly lit parlor of her well-kept home she told me how she had huddled for safety in the ranch buildings, how the storehouse had been plundered, how a call for help went out to the nearest town two hours distant and a posse of Model Ts arrived from Marfa just as the last armed horsemen disappeared toward the Rio Grande. She had watched as the corpse of one bandit, buried by his cohorts during a lull in their attack, was disinterred by the enraged Texans. "They stripped his uniform off and tied the body to the hood of a car," she said. "Riding back to Marfa with him there, all I could see was his bare back in the moonlight. To this day I've never thought moonlit nights were romantic."

North of Van Horn, at the end of a dirt road in the barren Sierra Diablo, ranch matriarch Mrs. J. V. McAdoo remembers with spellbinding clarity how she and her husband, in the morning of their lives, rode out in a covered wagon to find the land they made their own. On that land the last Indian battle in Texas was fought a generation before. As we drove together across her ranch, I noticed a symbol on the government's topographic map for an "archaeological site" nearby and asked her what it might be. "That," she said, "was our first home."

Texas has its man-made frontier artifacts like the "Alamo Village" outside Brackettville, carefully crafted for a movie set and now preserved for the amusement of tourists, but the real thing still exists here and there, in places like Candelaria. Those who expect swinging-door saloons and gun battles on dusty streets, though, will turn away disappointed. To a degree that may be beyond our imagining today, the frontier was often a place of solitude, of infinite possibility tinged with foreboding, wrapped in a mantle of silence.

Candelaria lies at the end of Texas Ranch Road 170, an hour's drive upriver from the ancient Rio Grande settlement of Presidio, itself a suitable candidate for the end of the earth. If you have made the trip without getting swept into a flash flood on one of the unbridged arroyos, your first thought will be to wonder whether you have actually arrived. The town consists of a high-ceilinged general store run by two elderly sisters named Nellie Howard and Marion Walker, a one-room schoolhouse partitioned by necessity into two, an unused jail that is more like an open-air cage, a Catholic church, and a few houses sheltered by broad cottonwood trees, all reduced to insignificance beneath the towering escarpment of the Sierra Vieja. In Candelaria nothing ever happens — except life and death.

When I last visited, one bright autumn morning, Nellie Howard stood behind the counter, her eyes glistening with tears. The day before, an old widower named Ramon Jasso had gone alone in the midday heat to chop mesquite on Capote Creek, and on the three mile homeward hike his seventy-seven-year-old heart gave out. Not until morning was he missed. Searchers found him beside the road, his armload of firewood splayed out where he had fallen. Marion Walker brought a cloth to cover his body and stood beside him in the desert until the sheriff and the hearse could make the sixty-mile journey from Presidio. In *Slouching Toward Bethlehem,* Joan Didion respectfully called this

Harlingen's Confederate Air Force, which keeps vintage war planes flying, reenacts World War II air battles in elaborate air shows.

sort of thing "wagon-train morality." In the Trans-Pecos, people still know what that means. "One of the promises we make to one another," Didion wrote, "is that we will try to retrieve our casualties, try not to abandon our dead to the coyotes. If we have been taught to keep our promises...we stay with the body, or have bad dreams." That is the frontier ethic you find in Candelaria.

At the schoolhouse, Johnnie Chambers, a rancher's wife, and Tip Chesney, a young man paid by the Migrant Program, teach two dozen Mexican children and serve jointly as scoutmasters for Candelaria's seven Boy Scouts. At recess, the children raced out the door, switching to Spanish the moment they crossed the threshold. Johnnie paused to catch her breath. "This is the only school most of these kids will ever see," she said. "Every once in a while you throw up your hands and say, what's the use. But you always want to try again. When you have a few successes, it's worth it." In eleven years, she has not taken a day of sick leave, and her graduates sometimes return from as far away as Midland to tell her of their careers. She called the children back with a hand-rung brass bell.

★

In urban Texas, churches promote themselves with Sunday-go-to-meeting enthusiasm in radio and television advertisements. In the Trans-Pecos, although the advent of cable is bringing new ways, television is not yet an obsession, and the ways of God and man are different, too. Nothing says more about religion there than the Bloys Camp Meeting, held by four Protestant denominations at a campground near Fort Davis each August since 1888. It combines family reunion with religious revival, and the old ranch families are its most dedicated supporters. Thousands come from miles around to socialize and attend religious services held four times daily at a central tabernacle. No fees are charged, photographs are discouraged, nothing can be bought or sold, and meals are served free to everyone at six great "eating sheds." There are dozens of individually owned cabins. Some are simple, others, elaborate. But like everything at Bloys, they are used just once a year. "Each family is always in the same place," the young Presbyterian minister in Fort Davis told me, "and everything is dependent on donations. At the end, after

the Treasurer's report, two cowboy hats are put on either side of the platform, and people go up and stick in a check for that year." The wish for rain being what it is, the most popular hymn is always "Showers of Blessing."

At such gatherings the West Texas rancher moves in his element. If at other times he seems on his guard, aloof, wincing at the outside world, the reason is not hard to find. For generations in this rugged country a stranger has meant trouble unless proven otherwise. The rancher instinctively divides the human species into two types: "good people" and "bad people," categories assumed to exist, fixed, in the nature of things. They measure not race or wealth or education, but a man's character, integrity, and moral fiber. What seems to be suspiciousness of outsiders is often the opening phase of an effort to size up a stranger and decide which category he fits. If the verdict is favorable, the wariness melts and a torrent of words pours forth, as if a stopper had been yanked from a reservoir of loneliness.

Alpine, with almost six thousand residents, a college, and a Safeway supermarket, is the closest thing to a metropolis the Trans-Pecos has. Not far from campus is the home of the late H. Allen Smith, the best-selling humorist who showed up in 1967 to represent New York in the first round of what has become the rambunctious Terlingua Chili Cookoff. With the din of Manhattan traffic still ringing in his ears, he climbed a hillside, looked west toward the mountains, and declared, "Right by God here. This is where I'm gonna live." Smith sold carloads of books by adopting the persona of an acid-tongued curmudgeon who made fun of everything, a technique that worked swimmingly on paper but one which soon made him *persona non grata* among his neighbors in straightforward, homespun Alpine.

A raucous bacchanalia in the desert, his chili festival continues each November. Like the Bloys Camp Meeting, the same people come back every year. When I dropped by to pay my respects at the 1982 bash, there were people dressed as cavemen chanting "Lone Star La-va," others dressed as gypsies, as airplanes, as surgeons selling "Sterile Chili." There were lanky men in long red underwear and mouse ears. There was Mount Saint Helens Chili and the Be-Bob Soda Shop and Judge Roy Bean and Mud Flap Chili. One visit to the Terlingua Cookoff, like one performance of *Parsifal*, might be enough to last a lifetime.

The Dallas State Fair Park, site of the country's largest annual state exposition, is also home to the Cotton Bowl.

The two big worries in the Trans-Pecos today are oil exploration and absentee land ownership. "We're off the beaten track," explains editor Bob Dillard of the *Alpine Avalanche* approvingly, "and the thing that could kill it quickest is oil. It may sound blasphemous to say this, but oil brings all kinds of bad things. It's a whole different way of life—fights, killings, a transient population. They come in and mess up the place and leave." The lure of oil and the traditional Texan prestige associated with ownership of land have priced many Texas ranches far beyond their productive value for cattle raising. Wealthy urbanites and corporate speculators tempt landowning families with deals they cannot refuse, not only in the Trans-Pecos but in the Hill Country west of Austin and in the rural environs of Houston. "The ranches," laments Dillard, "are the backbone of this country. If they get bought by the kind of guy who wants to play cowboy one weekend a month, what's going to become of us?"

Across from Happy Godbold's Feed Store in Marfa, encircled by a block-square, nine-foot adobe wall, sculptor Donald Judd is an improbable newcomer to these parts. Wearing wooden shoes and looking like a cross between Peter Ustinov and Buffalo Bill, he quieted his German shepherd dogs and walked me from his gate to a sparsely furnished room. Monteverdi played on the stereo and *The New York Times* lay on a table.

Judd advocates what he calls "permanent installations" of art. Museums and cluttered private homes are unsuitable, he argues: a work of art should be installed in a perfect uncrowded setting where it can stay undisturbed forever.

Such as Marfa? Yes, exactly. Aided by the Dia Foundation, Judd has spent years arranging his vast abstract sculptures in an abandoned aircraft hangar and the buildings of Fort Russell, a former cavalry post. Other artists may follow. "Not to be grand about it," he says, "when we're finished this will be the largest visible, permanent installation in the world. The Museum of Modern Art has more, of course, but lots of theirs are in the basement."

Because Judd finds it difficult to install even six works in one room satisfactorily, many of his are in the open country — great concrete blocks deposited among the grama grass and the grazing antelopes. "I can't get all of them out here either," he conceded, walking through a field near the Presidio highway. "But that's okay. It does get a little repetitious. Watch out for rattlesnakes."

The lush, well-watered grasslands around Marfa conform so closely to mind's-eye Texas that *Giant* was filmed there. But a hundred miles down US 90, at Sanderson, the land grows rocky, dry, and tough, and the sheep ranchers who congregate over a cup of coffee at the local cafe lead a different, harder life. Their spokesman, who has served in the state legislature, is a blunt, candid, rancher-businessman named Dudley Harrison. I first caught up with Dudley the weekend before he won his first term. The thoughts he has and the way he gives voice to them remind me why, in a country as big as the United States, Texas remains a different kind of place.

Without embarrassment he told how he went broke in the fifties. In the Trans-Pecos, bankruptcy is like drought: just one of those things that happen. Taking a job at the post office, he held on to become a Texaco distributor and get back on his feet again. Like every rancher I have ever met, he had no use for laws that tie his hands against coyotes, eagles, and other predators. "They say don't destroy the balance of nature," he snapped. "When God put man on earth, He destroyed the balance of nature." Like the stout-hearted frontiersmen who preceded him, his passion is to keep government at bay.

It was nine o'clock on a Saturday night when Dudley Harrison finished talking. His day had begun early, with trouble at a well on his ranch, and it was not over yet. There was scarcely time for politics. "But I went to the football game last night, just at sunset," he said, his voice suddenly subdued, "and there was a windmill silhouetted against the sky, and they were raising the Texas and American flags, and you could see the mountains off in the distance, and I thought, there's no place this good *anywhere*. I love it. I'm happy with who I am and I'm happy with where I live." Even if Sanderson did lose to Rankin, an oil town across the Pecos, 61 to 6.

★

When the French philosopher Alexis de Tocqueville visited America before the Civil War, the great westward migrations of the time impressed him deeply. "This gradual and continuous progress of the European race

Forested East Texas is culturally and topographically more akin to the deep South than to the ranchlands of West Texas.

Left: Master blacksmith Joe Stroud used the wall of his shop to test the branding irons he forged. Stroud founded the shop in Devine, south of San Antonio, in 1903 and ran it until his death in 1966; his son operates it today. *Above:* Just west of the Guadalupe Mountains lie the barren, windswept dunes of the Salt Flats. A dispute over these thick salt deposits flared into a brief border war in 1877.

Above: Agave lechuguilla manages to survive in the rock-strewn soil of the Hueco Mountains, which separate Diablo (Devil) Plateau from the El Paso area. *Right:* Mountain meets desert in Guadalupe Mountains National Park. McKittrick Canyon shelters one of the state's two stands of bigtooth maple, its only wild elk herd, and native rainbow trout. *Overleaf:* Downtown El Paso and the lights of Ciudad Juarez, Mexico's fourth-largest city, viewed from the Franklin Mountains.

Left: Texas, New Mexico, and Mexico converge northwest of El Paso at a mountain topped by a white limestone sculpture of Christ, which overlooks the area in Texas where Spanish settlements were established three centuries ago. *Above:* Canoeists brave the swirling rapids of Upper Madison Falls in the Lower Canyons of the Rio Grande. *Overleaf:* Among the haunting beauties of the Trans-Pecos is graceful, 150-foot Capote Falls, the state's highest waterfall.

Above: The rugged Chisos Mountains rise well over a mile above the desert floor. Beyond lies the South Rim, from which a one hundred-mile arc of the Rio Grande is visible. *Right:* U.S. 90 and Southern Pacific tracks bear eastward toward Alpine through terrain so forbidding the Spaniards called it the *Despoblado* —the unpopulated place. *Overleaf:* The river road between Big Bend National Park and Presidio passes eroded rock formations near Redford in the Bofecillos Mountains.

Left: A quicksilver boom once made Terlingua a thriving community. Today the ghost town west of Big Bend Park comes alive when revelers invade the desert for the world championship chili cookoff. *Above:* The Pronghorn antelope, native to the Trans-Pecos plains and North America's fastest mammal, is capable of sustained speeds of forty-five miles per hour. The Pronghorn's curiosity was its death warrant until state game officials limited hunting more than half a century ago.

Apaches, Kiowas, and Comanches once camped near the large natural cisterns in what is now Hueco Tanks State Park northeast of El Paso, leaving behind more than two thousand pictographs. Later, this oasis served as a watering hole for the Butterfield Overland Mail Route running between San Antonio and San Francisco.

In the spring and any time after a rain, the Chihuahuan Desert in West Texas bursts into bloom with plants like the rainbow cactus. Also know as *Echinocereus rigidissimus*, the rainbow cactus has flowers of many different colors.

A red-tailed hawk prepares to take off from a sotol stalk near Valentine in the Trans-Pecos. Sotol, or *Dasylirion,* is native to Mexico and the Southwestern United States. The early pioneers used sotol stalk to make roofs for their adobe houses.

Above: Traffic on Interstate 10 heads west toward El Paso and the Quitman Mountains. Erosion has loosened the soil's precarious grip; the hazy afternoon sky is the result of dust from overgrazing. *Overleaf:* In the late 1850s, westbound travelers on the Butterfield Overland Mail Route looked down from the Guadalupe Mountains on a vast desert of gypsum dunes and salt flats.

Above: A popular hike in the 700,000-acre Big Bend National Park leads to The Window, a portal in the Chisos Mountains high above the desert floor. *Right:* The isolation of the Trans-Pecos and the cool, clear air of the Davis Mountains are ideal conditions for surveying the heavens, a function superbly performed at the McDonald Observatory of the University of Texas near Fort Davis.

Left: Palo Duro Canyon, its formations sculpted by a fork of the Red River, is part of Texas' largest state park. *Above:* Rows of sunflowers turn their faces toward the rising sun on the plains near Lubbock. An important source of cooking oil, sunflowers need little water, making them an ideal crop for arid areas.

Palo Duro Canyon holds the layered geologic history of 200 million years. In 1876, legendary rancher Charles Goodnight drove a herd of cattle here and established the J. A. Ranch, becoming the first white man to settle the Panhandle.

Above: In Amarillo, capital of the Panhandle's oil and gas industry, a cowhand herds calves from stock pens to the auction block at the largest cattle auction in the world. *Overleaf:* Texas ranks among the top five states in wheat production, with half of its crop coming from the High Plains north of Amarillo.

Not all the fields in the Panhandle are wheat. Some of the state's richest oil and gas deposits lie under the fecund soil between Pampa and Perryton. Texas is the nation's top producer of oil and natural gas.

Cousin to the rare whooping crane that winters on the middle Texas coast, the sandhill crane abounds in the Panhandle and on prairies throughout Texas. Its migrations can be seen from March to May and from September to December.

Above: No image in Texas is more startling than these ten Cadillacs buried up to their fins on the plains west of Amarillo. The monument was commissioned in 1974 by eccentric local millionaire Stanley March 3 (never III). *Right:* The legendary Texas Rangers secured the frontier against Indian raiders on the west and Mexican bandits to the south. A bronze sculpture by Robert Summers immortalizes their story in the Texas Ranger Hall of Fame in Waco.

Left: Manmade lakes like Lake Texoma, north of Dallas, are important for recreation as well as conservation, power, and flood control. *Above:* The Texas Legislature designated the pecan the official state tree, chili the state dish, and the mockingbird, which here enjoys a barbed wire perch, the state bird. *Overleaf:* Reunion Tower dominates the sleek Dallas skyline. The Magnolia Building is topped by the neon Flying Red Horse, for thirty years the city's civic symbol.

Designed by architect Philip Johnson, the Fort Worth Water Gardens lie thirty-eight feet below street level, sealing out the city's noise with soothing waterfalls and fountains that pump nineteen thousand gallons per minute. The Water Gardens were built in a philanthropic resurgence during the 1970s that also produced the Kimbell Art Museum, designed by architect Louis Kahn.

Above: Dallas has long regarded itself as the cultural center of Texas. Its new downtown arts district is home to the Dallas Museum of Art, where Claes Olden-burg's sixteen-foot "Stake Hitch" is tied to the ceiling with a forty-foot rope. *Overleaf:* The Sabinal River reflects the glories of fall in Lost Maples State Park in the western Hill Country. Here, and in the Guadalupe Mountains far to the west, the state's only bigtooth maples signal the change of seasons.

A marble likeness of Stephen F. Austin, the empresario who received the original land grant to colonize Texas in 1821, surveys the entrance to the rotunda of the Texas Capitol in Austin. This statue was created by German immigrant Elisabet Ney. Her turn-of-the-century studio is now an Austin museum.

Above: The traditions of wildness and civilization merge in the rodeo, still a staple of life in small towns like Caldwell in Central Texas. *Overleaf:* Three Texas images: the tower of the University of Texas in Austin, the fountain of the Lyndon B. Johnson Presidential Library, and football. The football game, apparently, is about to conclude successfully for U. T. because orange lights, a signal of victory, already illuminate the top of the tower.

Above: The Winedale Historical Center, near Brenham. In 1940 more than half of all Texans lived on farms or in unincorporated rural settlements. Today 80 percent live in the state's twenty-six metropolitan areas, and the small farmer is passing into history. *Right:* West of Austin, the sun sets over Lake Travis.

Left: Texas has many caves, but only a few have been commercially developed. The largest of these is Natural Bridge Caverns near New Braunfels. *Above:* Only one state can boast that it was once a nation unto itself. The flag of the Republic of Texas flies with the flags of the five nations who have claimed Texas allegiance: the United States, the Confederacy, Mexico, Spain, and France.

Above: A turn-of-the-century tackroom at LBJ State Park, near the Hill Country of Fredericksburg. Early Texans took their horses seriously: horse thievery was often punished more severely than murder. *Right:* Fall foliage—here, bigtooth maples in Lost Maples State Park—is a rare sight in Texas, where most trees are perennially green. *Overleaf:* Bales of hay, tightly rolled to protect against the elements, are a common sight in springtime pastures.

Left: Gorman Falls begins as a spring a few yards from its precipice and tumbles over limestone into the Hill Country's Colorado River. *Above:* These peach blossoms will contribute to the state's deliciously tart peach crop, much of which is harvested near Stonewall, not far from the LBJ Ranch.

Farming in the Rio Grande Valley has destroyed the habitat of many native animals including the ocelot, a rare and endangered wild cat. This ocelot dwells in the Texas Zoo in Victoria, where all the animals are indigenous to Texas.

Above: Coursing through some of the most arid parts of Texas, the Rio Grande gives life to parched land. This tall, thick grass in ranch country below Laredo is a sure sign the river is not far away. *Overleaf:* Between the mouths of the Sabine and Rio Grande rivers lie more than three hundred miles of gulf shoreline. State law keeps virtually all Texas beaches open to the public.

Above: Hunting is a ritual in Texas; hunting leases are almost as prized as oil and gas leases. The preferred prey is the whitetailed deer, with birds like this wily Rio Grande turkey of Central and South Texas coming in a distant second. *Right:* The emblem on this Brownsville boy's cowboy hat reads, "Born of War," a slogan that could serve all of South Texas, where two cultures struggled for precedence.

Left: Sentinel for the southernmost tip of mainland Texas until 1905, the lighthouse at Port Isabel is now a state historic park beckoning tourists to the resort beaches of South Padre Island. *Above:* A 5,817-foot-long bridge spans the entrance to the port of Corpus Christi, the major oil terminal for South Texas.

Above: Onshore winds from the Gulf of Mexico twist coastal trees like this live oak near Corpus Christi into semaphores pointing inland. *Right:* Sheltered by lower Padre Island, a fleet of shrimp boats rests at the Port of Brownsville, fifteen miles east of the city. *Overleaf:* The bell towers of San Antonio's San Francisco de Espada, completed in 1745, are framed by the arch of what used to be its granary.

Left: The Texas shoreline begins its graceful eastward sweep halfway up the length of Padre Island, the world's longest barrier island, which includes resorts and a national seashore. *Right:* The Confederate Air Force, a group of thirty-six hundred "colonels" (the CAF's only rank) is devoted to keeping World War II planes like this B-17 Flying Fortress airworthy. Its annual air show attracts over 120,000 people.

Above: In the 1960s and 1970s, NASA's Lyndon B. Johnson Space Center near Houston served as mission control for the Apollo flights that sent man to the moon. Today's visitors can view lunar rock samples, spacecraft from actual NASA flights, and an astronaut's suit. *Right:* A tanker unloads imported crude oil at a Beaumont refinery. Because Texas ports are too shallow for supertankers, incoming oil is transferred into smaller tankers offshore.

Left: In the oil-rich Golden Triangle formed by Beaumont, Port Arthur, and Orange, these wells in the bayous of the Neches River are accessible only by boat and catwalk. *Above:* Two "roughnecks" struggle with machinery on a workover rig. For a few Texans, like former Governor Bill Clements, roughnecking was the first step to a fortune. *Overleaf:* What oil means to Houston's economy is written on the city's skyline. As oil prices climbed, so did the height of the buildings.

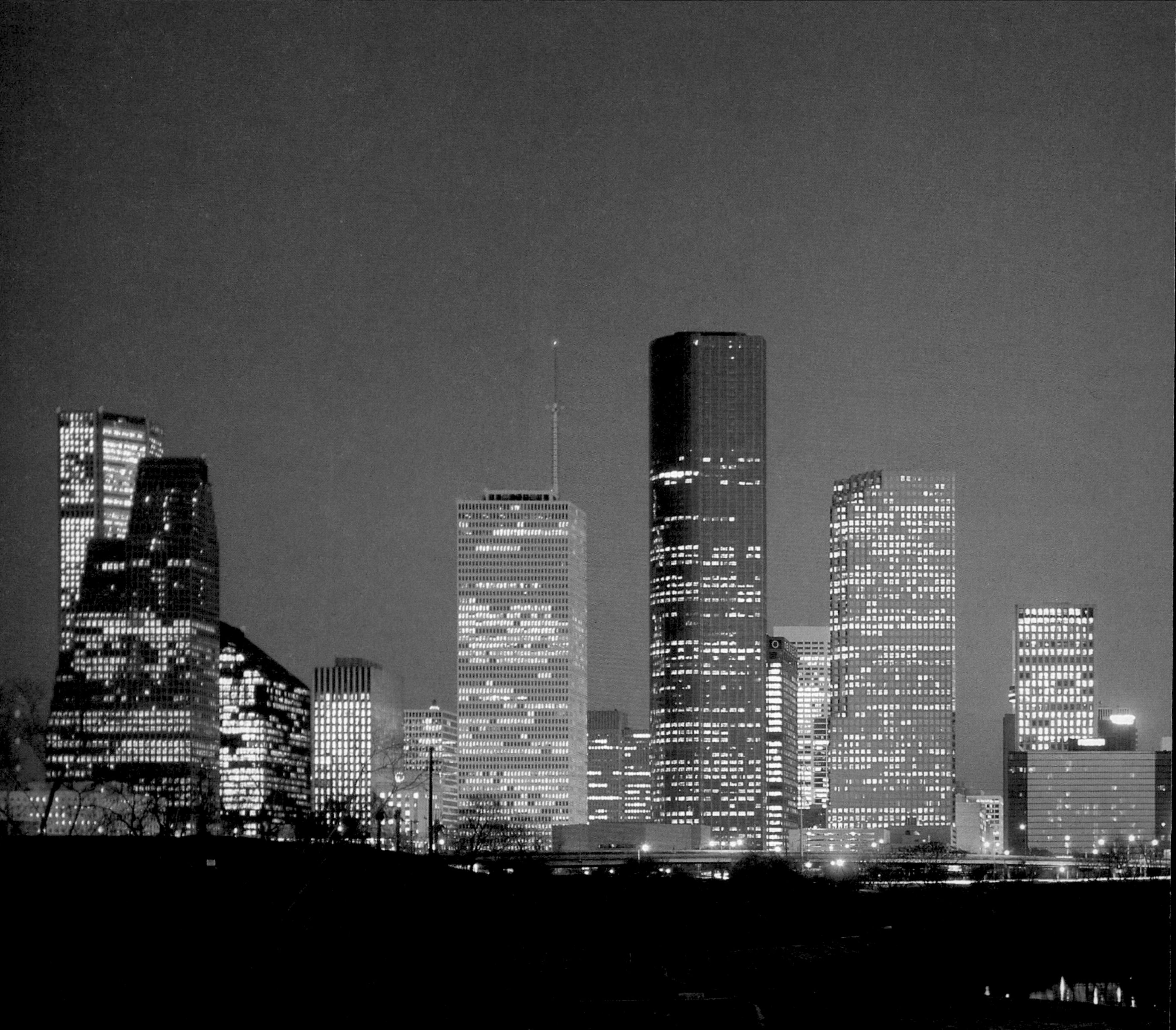

Seagulls—properly called laughing gulls—congregate on the shore of Galveston Island at sunrise. The historic city of sixty thousand people is now protected from the Gulf of Mexico by a seawall erected after a hurricane inundated the island and killed six thousand people in 1900. Two causeways and the state-operated Bolivar Ferry connect Galveston to the mainland.

A flooded rice field near Houston betrays no hint of the encroaching suburbia that
has overrun similar farmland. Since the record harvest of 1968, rice has declined
from third place to fifth among Texas crops as ricelands continue to disappear.

With its dense undergrowth, champion trees, impenetrable swamps, and abundant wildlife, the Big Thicket northwest of Beaumont is the essence of backwoods. Union sympathizers hid out in its eight hundred-square miles during the Civil War; moonshiners found it a sanctuary during Prohibition. Today it is favored by birders, who can locate the barred owl by its distinctive cry, "Who-cooks-for-you?"

The Big Thicket is a botanical crossroads in East Texas. It is home to desert cacti and tropical plants like the carniverous jack-in-the-pulpit. It is also prime logging country. Following a lengthy battle between environmentalists and timber companies, 84,500 acres were set aside as the Big Thicket Natural Preserve.

The tidal wetlands near Port Arthur are breeding grounds for ducks, geese, musk-rats, wading birds, alligators, shrimp, and fish—and sanctuary for squatters' shacks like the hunter's cabin in the foreground. These are built on public land but by tradition are considered private property.

Above: World War II cargo ships lie mothballed in the Neches River near Beaumont, a center of the chemical and petrochemical industries. On January 10, 1901, in the nearby Spindletop Oil Field, the first great Texas oil well blew. *Overleaf:* With its muddy banks and thick, decaying vegetation, Blue Elbow Swamp near Orange is a piece of southern Louisiana transplanted to Texas.

Deep in East Texas, a logging road winds through a pine forest near San Augustine. The forty-three counties hidden beneath the Piney Woods scarcely resemble the Texas of myth: they are southern, rainy, and poor. Local timber barons maintained "company towns" well into the post-World War II era.

Residents of the Piney Woods do not have to go to Houston or Dallas to visit a zoo. This peacock is showing its colors at the Ellen Trout Zoo in Lufkin, a timber and industrial center with a population of twenty-eight thousand.

Manmade reservoirs like Lake Livingston on the Trinity River have opened new recreational opportunities to timber-bound East Texans, giving them an opportunity to view the full Texas sky, as well as to sail, swim, and fish.

A little green heron searches for prey from a fence post in the Anahuac National Wildlife Refuge. Located approximately thirty miles east of Houston in Chambers County, this refuge is typical of Gulf Coast marshland.

Less than three miles from the city limits of Orange, moss-draped cypress and tupelo border the Sabine River and Blue Elbow Swamp. No loggers operate here; this is the primeval domain of the snake, the bullfrog, the sea turtle, and the beaver. Orange itself boasts the Stark Museum of Art, which includes major exhibits depicting the West's land, wildlife, and people; an American Indian collection; Audubon prints; and bronzes by Frederick Remington.

Above: A Louisiana heron inspects the coastal marshes of the Anahuac National Wildlife Refuge, which is a sanctuary for ducks, geese, alligators, and more than two hundred and fifty species of waterfowl. *Overleaf:* The Astrodome, the nation's first domed sports stadium, opened in Houston in 1965 and is the home of the baseball Astros and football Oilers.

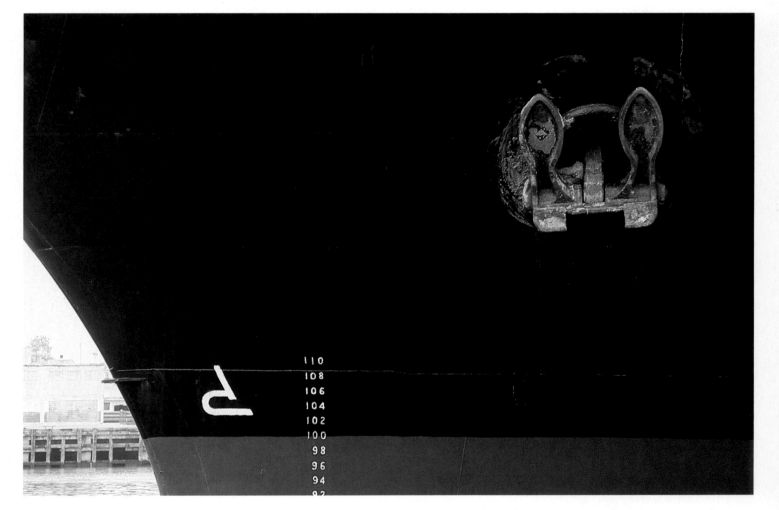

Above: Its anchor hoisted, a moored freighter rides high in the water. Now the nation's third-largest port, inland Houston had no access to deep water until 1914, when local boosters dredged sluggish Buffalo Bayou to reach Galveston Bay. *Right:* The 570-foot San Jacinto Monument, near Houston, is higher than the Washington Monument—as any Texan will tell you — and commemorates the 1836 battle at which Texas won its independence from Mexico.

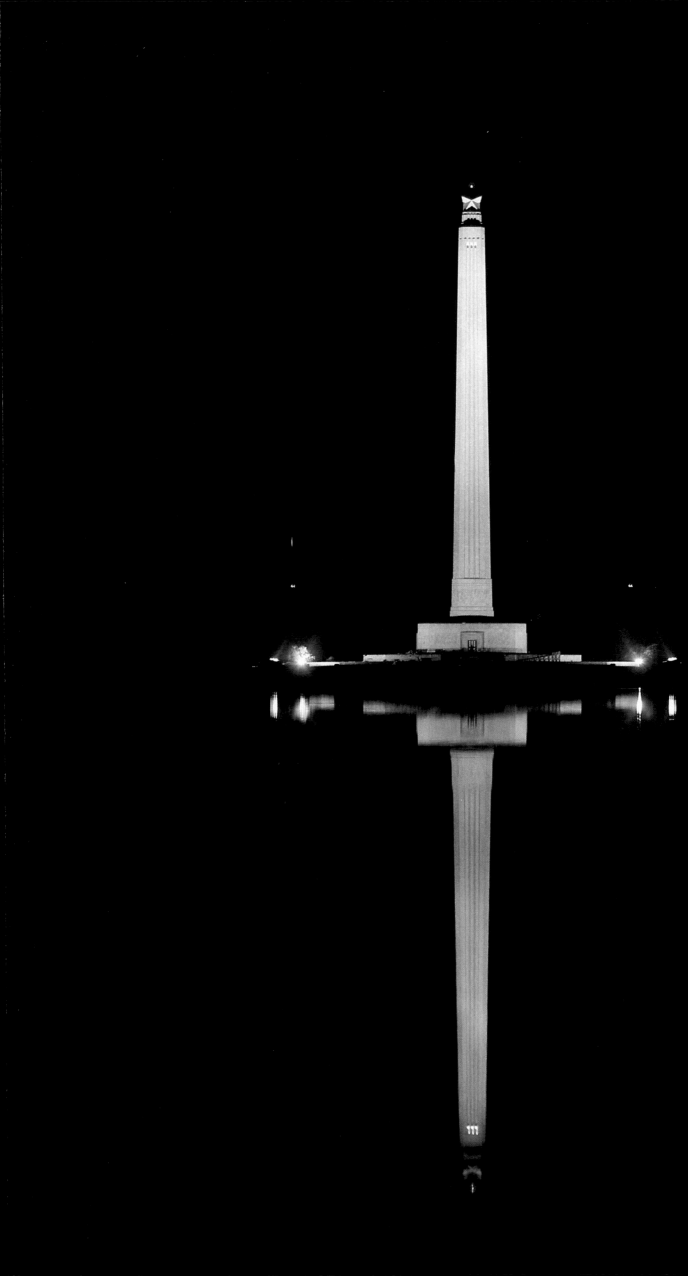

Left: The derrick is a disappearing sight in the oil patch, where modern wells are drilled with portable rigs. Here, an old well is still producing oil near Orange.
Above: To remove the oil and mud after a day in the oil fields east of Houston, this roughneck had to scrub himself with kerosene.

Fishing for crappie in Lake Livingston, seventy-five miles north of Houston.
Crappie prefer fertile lakes and build nests which the males defend pugnaciously.
East Texas is also a landscape of red-earth farms, pine forests, and pioneer towns.

Above: A portable rig drills a well in the Austin Chalk formation near La Grange in Central Texas. The weekly "rig count," which measures the number of oil and gas wells being drilled, is the most important economic indicator in Texas. *Overleaf:* Between downtown Houston and the San Jacinto battleground, the Houston Ship Channel is bordered by an eerie landscape of towers, tanks, and steam.

Above: Galveston's Historic District features ornate nineteenth century homes from the era when the island port was the most important city between New Orleans and San Francisco. *Right:* Remote Matagorda Island on the Central Texas coast, is accessible only by boat or aircraft. Half the island is a park; the other half is a cattle ranch. While urban Texas strives for world eminence, rural Texas still marches to a different drum.